TRACKING
WILD CHIMPANZEES

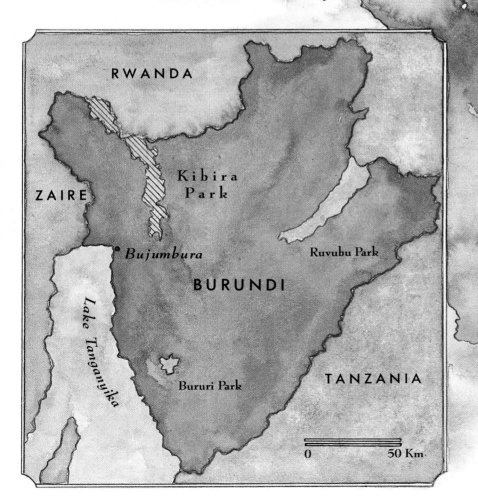

Sahara Desert

Sudan

Upper Guinea

SOUTH ATLANTIC OCEAN

Ethiopian Highlands

Somali Peninsula

Congo Basin

Lake Victoria

BURUNDI

Lake Tanganyika

Lake Malawi

Kalahari Desert

Mozambique Channel

MADAGASCAR

INDIAN OCEAN

RWANDA

ZAIRE

Kibira Park

Bujumbura

Ruvubu Park

BURUNDI

Lake Tanganyika

Bururi Park

TANZANIA

0   50 Km

For my mentor, Eleanor.

I WISH TO THANK the National Museum in Nairobi, Kenya, for allowing me to study and paint from their bird collection. I am especially indebted to Pete Trenchard and Jill Reisschneider, who were so generous with their time, and to Stephen Henri Devoto for his unending support.

Library of Congress Cataloging in Publication Data Powzyk, Joyce Ann. Tracking wild chimpanzees/by Joyce Powzyk. p. cm. Summary: The author describes her visit to The Kibira National Park to see chimpanzees, and shares her observations of people, culture, and wildlife in Burundi as well. ISBN 0-688-06733-6. ISBN 0-688-06734-4 (lib. bdg.) 1. Chimpanzees—Juvenile literature. [1. Burundi—Description and travel. 2. Chimpanzees.] I. Title QL737.P96P69 1988 599.88'44—dc19 87-16099. CIP. AC.

JOYCE POWZYK

TRACKING
WILD CHIMPANZEES

IN KIBIRA NATIONAL PARK

LOTHROP, LEE & SHEPARD BOOKS   NEW YORK

ONE · ARRIVAL

My plane touched down on the small runway's tarmac. I was in Bujumbura, the capital city of Burundi, tucked away between Rwanda and Tanzania, along Lake Tanganyika. The official language of Burundi is French because the country was a Belgian colony until it was declared a republic in 1962.

We had landed on what is known as the Rusizi Plain. At the turn of the twentieth century this was reported to be a "paradise" of animal life, with large numbers of duiker, bush pig, monkeys, and occasionally black leopard. They lived in a rich habitat of grass and trees watered by the country's plentiful rainfall. Judging from the crops I had seen from the air, the plain was now an important agricultural area.

Stepping off the plane, I saw Pete, a friend from college. He looked just as I remembered him from our days as biology students back in Illinois. We exchanged waves as I headed to the immigration desk, where my passport was checked and stamped. I had come to see the chimpanzees of the Kibira National Park, where Pete was conducting a wildlife census. *Kibira* is the word for forest in the native Kirundi language.

"Hello there, stranger! It's good to see you," Pete greeted me. "You were lucky I was in Bujumbura to get your telegram. You haven't changed a bit."

We walked out to the truck and threw my gear in the back. "Thought we might head straight up to my house in the forest. Bujumbura makes me uneasy, too much of a city," said Pete. I mumbled a response, but my gaze was immediately caught by all the color and bustle of Bujumbura. Ebony-skinned women with brightly patterned fabric wrapped about their bodies waited at the bus stops. I watched in amazement as the women carried large baskets or earthenware pots so effortlessly on their heads, using just one hand for guidance.

"Today is *marché* day," added Pete. "We'll stop by the market in Kayanza."

We passed through Bujumbura and stopped to inquire about a piece of equipment. People were selling items outside the butcher's shop, and I paused to look at several different types of orchids and ferns. A young boy ran up and surprised me with his offer of two helmeted guinea fowl, one in each hand, dangling by their feet. Pete smiled as he declined to buy the birds, and said we would have something different for dinner.

We soon departed Bujumbura, climbing above the plains into the steep mountain-hills.

TWO·UP COUNTRY

The road twisted and turned back on itself as we followed the route north. Eucalyptus trees had been planted as guard rails, to prevent vehicles from veering off the steep embankment. Everywhere I looked was a landscape of green and fertile farmland.

Villagers walked along the roadside. Several women labored with enormous loads of firewood strapped to their backs; the wood is used to cook the family meals. It was noontime, and groups of uniformed schoolchildren headed home, playing tag or pushing old wheels along with sticks.

We passed through small towns with names like Bukeye (boo-KAY-ee) and Bugarama (boo-ga-ra-ma). Many of the buildings appeared to barely cling onto the steep mountain slopes, with the family gardens running down vertically, away from the circular huts. I recognized beans, cabbages, corn, and stands of banana trees. The view down into the valley grew more picturesque.

We turned onto a new road, cut out from the side of the mountain. A high bank of bright red soil was exposed like an open wound. Without warning, a man on a bicycle flew by us, yelling as he missed our truck by inches. He had reams of green bananas stacked and tied to his bike.

"That man probably conducts his banana business on his bicycle, transporting goods to the *marché*," commented Pete. I settled back in my seat, prepared for the rest of the journey.

Finally we arrived in Kayanza. The town is located on top of a mountain. It sprawled out from its center point, the governor's office with its two flagpoles. People filled the streets and reluctantly let our truck pass as they talked and socialized.

"We'll park here and go into the market," said Pete, pointing up toward a huge gathering of people on the hill. The sight of hundreds of people mingling and showing their goods was spectacular. As I wandered into the market, people looked up from their baskets of manioc and papaya to stare and smile. My eyes feasted on the local produce. The sweet potatoes were long, purplish roots, and Pete remarked how tasty they were when boiled. The merchants offering salt for sale had carefully poured out identical piles onto a table.

We moved past loaves of bread, butchers with goat meat, rice, homemade rakes and hammers, fabric, and even plastic bowls. By this time a small group of children had gathered and followed us as we moved through the market. Every time we turned around, they laughed and covered their smiling faces with their hands. We came to a group of women selling baskets and I stopped to admire them. Each one had a unique design of blue and green reed woven into the lid. We bartered, and I soon carried out a beautiful basket for only 200 Burundi francs (about two American dollars). The women were delighted with this high price, which to me was a bargain. Pete bought food staples—flour, dry milk, sugar, and some bananas. We put the provisions into the truck and headed up country.

We passed by a church and a large tea plantation with several hundred hectares of tea plants. The glossy green leaves looked as if they were just waiting to be picked. The air was much cooler here in the mountains. Mosquitos would not be so bothersome.

Pete turned off the main road and we traveled down a narrow, rocky road, which wound its way to the valley floor. He honked the horn at each hairpin turn, warning people of our speedy approach. Finally we pulled up in front of a small red and white house. "Home," announced Pete.

THREE · BUSHWHACKING

The house was quaint. In the back was a small kitchen where André, the cook, spent most of his time preparing food. There was no running water or electricity.

I unloaded the vehicle, setting my belongings in the office, which was now my room. All my gear had arrived safely, including my camera and painting supplies. We lit several kerosene lanterns, as the sun had already set behind the mountains.

The evening was spent talking of Burundi and the Kibira Park. The land was set aside as a protected area in 1980, and one of Pete's jobs is to conduct a wildlife inventory—recording animal species that are found in the forest. His second job is to observe a population of wild chimpanzees that live in the Kibira. We made plans to get up a little before dawn. I was eager to see a central African montane rain forest with its vast diversity of plant and animal life.

I awoke to hear Pete shuffling about the house. Several candles were lit, as the sky was still dark. I pulled on my khaki pants and long-sleeved shirt and headed to the kitchen. The water was already boiling, so I made us both a cup of Burundi tea.

Going into the forest meant wearing suitable clothing with layers of undershirts, shirts, and rain gear, ready for any change in weather. Brightly colored clothes had to be avoided because chimps have good color vision. Central Africa was now in its wet season, and we were sure to encounter muddy trails and rain-swollen rivers.

I gathered everything together and we loaded ourselves onto Pete's motorcycle. The early morning light was beginning to spread across the little valley. From several huts nearby I saw smoke rising up over the roofs. The morning fires had been lit.

We headed up the winding dirt road, our headlight dancing before us. Once out on the main road, we passed shadowy figures of people making their way to the tea fields. Candles burned in the houses we passed, and I could see people inside, wrapped in blankets as they gathered around the stoves. We motored along until we came to the edge of the forest.

"We'll park the bike here and lock up our helmets," suggested Pete. "This is trail number two and I often see chimps here. There's lots of good eating when the fig trees are fruiting."

As we neared the forest, a narrow path leading into the darkness opened up what had appeared to be an impenetrable fortress of trees. I spotted a wild cucumber that had fallen to the ground—a favorite food of monkeys. I placed it in my field bag to examine later. The vegetation was dripping with moisture, and my clothes were instantly soaked. Inside the forest the upper branches and leaves created a thick canopy, preventing light from filtering through. The air smelled like tea brewing, probably from all the rotting leaves on the ground. But it was a clean smell, the smell of a living forest.

There were tree frogs croaking as we plodded along the muddy footpath. Pete and I had stopped to listen when I felt a sharp bite on my ankle. I was standing in a column of black safari ants. The scouts had large mandibles and they were desperately trying to bite me as they clung onto my trouser leg, twisting the material. Jumping out of the way, I knocked off all the ants I could see and hoped none had found their way to my bare skin.

Wild Cucumber

Pete continued along the trail and then halted in his tracks. All I could hear was a soft, birdlike chirping noise, but Pete whispered, "Blues." It took Pete's keen ear to recognize the sound as the call of a blue monkey. We broke off the trail and moved quietly through the forest, coming to a stand of bamboo. The branches were bobbing and swaying. "Only a primate can bend a branch like that," declared Pete. We spotted a large male blue monkey and heard an explosive "PIAO" sound, which was his warning call.

Blue Monkeys

Several younger monkeys were perched in the tops of the bamboo trees, eating leaves. They were beautiful creatures with coats of dark blue-gray fur. Each face had a white line across the eyebrows, accentuating the expression. One monkey was curious and stayed in view, watching us. He repeatedly stood up, looked at us, picked some leaves, and threw them down while nervously glancing back to his troopmates.

Gradually the monkeys moved off, the large male being the last to disappear into the green jungle. We backtracked to the main trail and I caught a glimpse of a black-billed turaco. The bird's green plumage blended perfectly into its leafy backdrop. The turaco was shy and hid behind a tree limb, bending its neck to take a look at us.

Black-billed Turaco

Trail two took us deeper into the forest. A magnificent mahogany tree measuring over a meter in diameter loomed ahead. Most of the country's hardwoods have been lumbered, except for those within the confines of the park. We came to a small cliff, overgrown with broad-leafed plants and flowering impatiens. A group of black-crowned waxbills flitted through the greenery, searching for seeds. We sat down and took a rest. I spied through the binoculars, scouting for chimps, but could see only a wall of dense foliage. What had been a cool, damp morning was beginning to warm up.

Black-crowned Waxbills

From somewhere in front of us came muffled screams. "Those are definitely chimpanzees!" exclaimed Pete.

Soon there was a chorus of noises. The chimps sounded excited and there were loud shrieks and soft whining calls all jumbled together. Pete and I hurried along the trail and then cut through the forest, following the chimps' calls.

Pete muttered, "They sound as if they're on the move, probably making a row because of the good change in weather."

Chimp Nest

Strombosia Fruits

We maneuvered between the scrub and young trees, not wanting to chop our way through with the machete because of the noise it would create. Our progress was slow as we headed down toward a ravine. Stinging nettles were everywhere and I was quickly reminded to put on my gloves. Hiking on the path had been easy, except for the mud, but now vines and roots grabbed at my feet, sending me stumbling forward. The chimps' loud outburst died down as abruptly as it had started. We continued to move in the same direction and after an hour picked up their trail. The area was thick with Strombosia trees; their ripe and rotting fruit covered the forest floor.

"The chimps obviously spent a good deal of time here, judging from the half-eaten fruits and broken foliage," Pete observed.

There were signs of chimpanzees everywhere. I studied discarded fruit and could see tooth marks where the chimps had scraped away the flesh from the large seeds. Broken tree limbs were all about, probably remnants from a playing spree. Pete found chimp spoor and collected it for examination later.

Above us in the branches were several chimp nests, which are made each night for sleeping. Chimps construct the nests by bending branches to form a strong platform, which they make comfortable with gathered leaves. The old nests were brown and breaking apart, but the newer nests had green leaves and fresh branches.

We were not able to determine how many chimps were in this particular band, but we did find their fresh trail leading farther down into the ravine. It was too late in the afternoon to continue tracking, so we reluctantly headed back to the house. Tomorrow would be a long day.

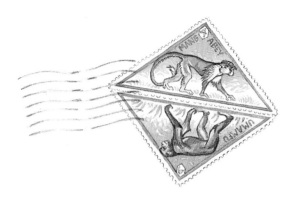

FOUR · "IMAMFU"

By daybreak we were back in the forest. A lone man carrying a bundle of goods stumbled on us as we hiked along the path. His face showed his surprise at seeing us. Pete asked if he had heard the *imamfu,* the Kirundi word for chimpanzee. He shook his head, waving his hand in the direction from which he had come.

Pete pulled out his machete and slashed through the vegetation, taking a shortcut to where we had left the chimps' trail. We followed the signs of bent grass and broken branches left by the chimps as they traveled along the ground. At one point the individuals of the band had separated and each had gone its own way, only to rejoin about twenty meters beyond. It became more difficult for us to move because of fallen trees that littered the ground. Our feet slipped between logs and we were constantly pulling ourselves out.

An early morning fog surrounded us as we moved closer to a small stream at the bottom of the ravine. We tracked the chimps through the watercourse and found a clear knuckle print an adult had left in the mud. There was also a good impression of a hind foot, showing the long pad and each toe. Farther downstream Pete noticed a cloven hoofprint, which was from either a bush pig or a giant forest hog.

We quit bushwhacking and crawled on our bellies, just as the chimps had done, beneath a thicket that was too tangled to advance through. "Watch out for the green mambas," muttered Pete. I realized this would not be an ideal time to encounter one of the most poisonous snakes of the Kibira Forest.

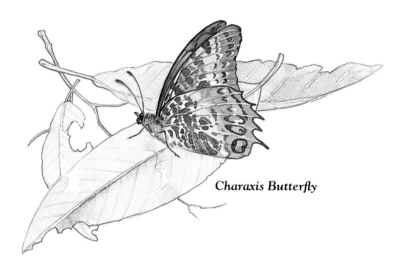

Charaxis Butterfly

Following the tracks, we climbed up the other side of the ravine into a group of Chrysophylum trees.

"A chimp could be right over your head, staring down at you without uttering a sound," Pete cautioned. "I always see the most when I just sit still and watch things move around me."

Pete has spent months tracking chimps, sighting them for a brief moment or sitting with them for hours as they have gone about their daily tasks. Now, movement in the branches quickly attracted Pete's attention. He pointed to the place, and after focusing my binoculars I saw a small chimpanzee playing out on a limb. The youngster appeared oblivious of our presence and was grabbing leaves and stuffing them into its mouth.

Pete whispered, "The mother is there too."

I scanned the tree and saw a large dark shape behind the youngster. She had seen us from the start. The band had to be close by, but for some reason this female had shunned their protection. Suddenly she moved. She grabbed her unsuspecting youngster and, without a sound, shinnied down the trunk of the tree. They both vanished into the five-foot stand of weeds below.

"We won't see any more of her," stated Pete. "She is extremely protective of that baby."

I was exhilarated. That was a wild chimpanzee, one that had never known the confines of a zoo. Along with her relations, this female chimp had roamed the wilds of Burundi and survived, even with the threat of human encroachment. The mother had certainly made a fast getaway. I had never realized how quiet chimps could be. My mental picture of wild chimpanzees was of screaming, raucous animals—ruling the forest they inhabited.

We picked up the path and hiked along, followed by a cloud of sweat flies. I was still thinking about the baby chimp when we heard some crashing noises. Once again the forest concealed its inhabitants, and Pete and I strained to see through the lush foliage. Finally we spotted them, grey-cheeked mangabeys, moving below us on the slope. The monkeys' faces were almost black and I could barely make out their eyes and mouths. Their bodies were also dark but I could see their distinguishing long fur, which flowed from their shoulders as they leapt to safety. I counted six adult mangabeys with two juveniles in this troop. Today the forest seemed full of primates.

Grey-cheeked Mangabey

Imbabura

Dusk was upon us when we arrived back at the house. We had spent a total of nine hours in the forest. Our daily forays were proving to be hard, exhausting work.

As on most evenings, I warmed up the lunch André had left. I took the small, portable stove called an *imbabura* (im-ba-BOO-rah) behind the house, loaded it with charcoal, and poured on a little kerosene. After lighting the charcoal, I swung the imbabura around by its handle, its contents kept in by centrifugal force while the flame was fed plenty of oxygen. The coals glowed bright orange as I peered up into the night. It was too early for Halley's comet to appear above the valley's ridge. We had been fortunate to find flour in the market, so tonight there was a jam torte along with the usual rice and sausages to celebrate our sighting of the chimps.

After dinner Pete and I discussed the park and how important the forest was to the surrounding agricultural areas. The 40,000 hectares of trees act as a watershed, absorbing rainfall like a sponge and sending it spewing off to the neighboring farms and gardens. The cultivated land is nourished from these waters and the Burundians benefit from the tracts of forest that are left intact.

We plotted the chimps' location on the map and talked of their movements. Chimpanzees will stay in one area for weeks, moving on when the food supply is exhausted. They often move from tree to tree, following their preferred fruit as it ripens. The pattern of their movements within the Kibira is not fully known, partially because they can be so difficult to track. These were the long-haired chimpanzees, *Pan troglodytes,* subspecies *schweinfurthi,* which are also found in West Tanzania and Central Africa. Pete proceeded to dissect the spoor he had collected. It contained the usual seeds and leaves from bamboo, wild banana, and fig trees—staples of the chimp's diet.

"I always check the spoor for any small bones or hair, to see if the chimps have been eating meat. Now we need to locate the main group," remarked Pete. "They can't elude us much longer."

FIVE · THE RAINS

The chimps did elude us, however. When we awoke the next morning it was raining, and it continued to rain for two days. The downpour was so heavy that mud splattered against the white walls of Pete's house and turned them brown.

I took the opportunity to sketch and paint all the vegetation I had collected from the forest and started to identify the major plant and tree species. There were other animals to learn about. Pete was always trying to track down reports of unfamiliar species sighted by the villagers. Africa during the rainy season is a difficult place to do field research.

The third day brought blue skies. A pair of Hadada ibis trumpeted their call in honor of the fair weather as they returned to their roost near the house. Pete and I immediately headed out to the stand of trees where we had sighted the mother and baby chimpanzee. The group might have moved during the bad weather, but we found signs that they were close by. The weeds were packed down where the chimps had sat while foraging for nuts and berries.

Then there was a whimper, directly in front us. It grew from a soft "ho, ho, ho" to a loud "ha, ha, ha, wraah, wraah!" We had taken a young chimp by surprise, and this was its panic call to the rest of the group, which remained hidden. Hoots and shrieks arose from the other chimps and then everything became quiet. A loud thumping noise sounded from the dense underbrush. A chimp was coming toward us, crashing through the foliage, breaking branches as it charged. Five meters away, a large male broke from the bushes and stopped. His elbows were thrust forward in a strut position and his hair stood on end, making him seem larger than life.

Our gazes met for just a few seconds, then he ran across the path. Others quickly followed—five chimps total.

We did not go after the chimps because we didn't want them to feel pursued. But Pete and I were determined, and the next day we located the same band. This time we stood out in the open. The chimpanzees could easily see us and showed no alarm. There appeared to be several more chimps in the group, but it is not uncommon for individuals to come and go between bands. Pete felt that all the chimpanzees were part of a large, interrelated Kibira population. *

"Just stay as quiet as you can," whispered Pete.

The brushes rustled and we watched a young chimp scamper quickly across an opening in the vegetation. I followed Pete's example and slowly started to climb a tree. Imitating their actions helps to keep the chimps calm. When we had found suitable positions, Pete and I settled into picking leaves, nibbling on twigs, and grooming ourselves. Direct eye contact with the chimps was avoided, except for a few seconds at a time. From the number of rustling bushes, we estimated the group to be seven chimps.

Finally, after an hour, an older male with silver hairs on his chin stayed out in the open to feed on bamboo. He cracked the stalk and tore out the pithy interior, chewing it till the moisture and taste were gone. He then spit out a round bundle of bamboo fibers. Pete refers to such bundles as "chimp chews."

Chimp Chews

*In 1986, the Kibira population of long-haired chimpanzees was estimated to be two hundred individuals.

21

Giant Forest Squirrel

A giant forest squirrel bounded noisily through the bamboo. It caught sight of us and froze into position with its tail arched over its back for balance. The old chimp took little notice of the intruder and continued to feed.

Our attention was drawn to a Myrianthus tree. An adult male emerged onto a branch, hastily eating away at something clutched in his hands. Two juveniles screamed as they tried to nuzzle in, but the chimp turned his back on them and continued to eat. When he turned again, I caught sight of something red. It was a small chunk of meat with some gray-green fur still attached. The fur resembled that of a baboon. The persistent youngsters badgered the older chimp till he spit out a morsel of meat into their palms. The two juveniles immediately hurried off to consume their prize, while the old male picked a few leaves and chewed them with the remaining meat.

Meat-eating by chimpanzees has been well documented in Africa. Baboons and chimps sometimes forage in the same area. This makes it possible for a group of chimps to hunt down a young baboon and kill it. Young chimpanzees who experience a kill and the eating of meat may grow up to continue the hunting tradition.

Several branches obstructed our view of the chimps, but to our surprise a curious female climbed up a neighboring tree to better observe the commotion and us. She had a baby clasped to her chest, and it stared wide-eyed at me and Pete. Her young one was about two years old, as indicated by the clump of white fur on its rump. The baby began to climb through the branches, testing the strength of its arms and legs. I glanced at them for short periods of time. The mother seemed unconcerned and leaned out to watch the other chimps. After the disturbance quieted down, she nestled the baby back to her belly, slid down the tree, and disappeared.

We spent a total of three hours with the chimpanzees. They ambled off after taking a midafternoon rest period of social grooming. The highest ranking male departed first and the others followed, single file. I realized my legs were badly cramped from sitting in the tree, yet the time had passed so quickly.

We observed the chimps many times after that. When it rained, they often sat in the downpour for hours without ever seeking cover. Their long coarse hair allowed the moisture to drip off, keeping the undercoat dry. We spied on several juveniles while they tried to construct day nests, as they had seen their elders do. The chimps' facial expressions were especially intriguing due in part to muscle and skeletal structures similar to those of humans. Wide eyes and pursed lips meant excitement, while uneasiness or fear was indicated by a grimace.

The behavior of chimpanzees has given biologists great insights into human evolution and primate behavior as a whole. Over 15 million years ago ancestral humankind and primates deviated from a common anthropoid, yet today we share 99 percent of our genetic material with the chimpanzee.

SIX · DEPARTURE

On my last day in the Kibira, Pete and I decided to hike to the eastern limit of the forest. Passing through the jungle en route, we sighted a troop of Angolan black and white colobus monkeys. They moved through the upper branches of the tallest trees, which were over thirty meters in height. We marveled at their acrobatic leaps as they landed powerfully on the swaying branches. Two young colobus stopped momentarily to watch us. They grabbed each other in a fit of playful tickling and then they were gone.

Angolan Black and White Colobus Monkeys

The Angolan colobus is always found in the upper canopy niche and seldom moves down to the lower levels of the forest. Blue monkeys prefer the middle canopy but occasionally wander to the edge area—the border between two habitats.

Pete and I approached the forest's edge, which consists of a few trees and bushes, flanked by farmland. A group of slender-billed chestnut-wing starlings flew by, their crimson patches flashing color as they cavorted in the wind. This edge area offered a different array of plants and animals from those we had grown familiar with in the dense jungle.

Near the trail we came across a feeding site where monkeys had been digging up grubs and plant tubers. We proceeded on and surprised several olive baboons in the tall grass. They immediately screamed and barked and took refuge in a nearby tree, which began to break under their weight.

The baboons were powerful animals, the older individuals weighing well over twenty-five kilos. A male yawned and showed us his long, yellow canine teeth, a nervous threat meant to keep us from approaching any closer. Olive baboons are commonly found in this open habitat. As a group they can be strong enough to fight off the leopard, their one natural enemy, though most of the big cats are gone.

Olive Baboons

We returned through the forest and stumbled upon a giant rat de Gambie caught by its tail in a wire noose. Pete released it and destroyed the illegal snare. Trapping is a remnant of the old tradition of taking food from the forest. Now the forest is too small to provide much food. The Kibira does maintain a wealth of birds, over a hundred and sixty species, as well as small mammals, reptiles, and primates. But most of the large forest antelopes, along with the carnivores, have been hunted or driven out.

Giant Rat de Gambie and snare

The skies darkened and it started to rain as we came to a rushing stream, flooded from the wet season. We quickly put on our ponchos as the thunder boomed overhead. It was fitting that my last day in the Kibira would be a drencher. Through the mist Pete and I saw a lone l'Hoest's monkey standing on its hind legs, carefully measuring out each leap between the exposed rocks. It was an adult male, his fur soaked and dripping with rainwater.

This handsome species of monkey has a large home range, and this one was exploring a different part of its territory for new food sources. The l'Hoest's monkey will often come down to the ground to forage or cross open areas, unlike the blue and colobus monkeys we had seen earlier. From my observations in the forest, I had seen how each species of monkey occupies a different ecological niche.

I would soon be departing Burundi and was glad to have seen for myself how the dense jungle of Kibira National Park is an invaluable natural resource. It is home to a cauldron of native plants and animals, including six species of higher primates—a surprisingly high diversity for a small reserve. The Kibira National Park is the largest area of montane rain forest remaining in Burundi today.

Epilogue

The benefits of maintaining tracts of rain forest are now widely acknowledged on both a local and global scale. Their vast oxygen-producing potential, along with the ability to lessen the effects of seasonal droughts and other climatic variances, can no longer be taken for granted, especially at the rate rain forests continue to be cut.

L'Hoest's Monkey

GLOSSARY

ANTHROPOID: resembling human or ape.

BIOLOGIST: one who studies living organisms—both plant and animal.

CANOPY: the dense spreading branches of a forest that form a continuous mat of vegetation.

CARNIVORE: meat eater.

DAY NEST: a nest of leaves and branches constructed by chimpanzees for use during the day, usually for napping.

DUIKER: small African antelope.

ECOLOGICAL NICHE: the combination of specific conditions (temperature, humidity, habitat) where a species can live and reproduce.

EDGE AREA: the border between two different habitats.

FORAGE: to search for food.

GENETIC MATERIAL: DNA sequences that provide the basic information determining the physical characteristics of a species. (99 percent of the DNA sequence of chimpanzee genes match sequences of human genes.)

GRUB: an insect's wormlike larva.

HABITAT: the physical environment, including the organisms that live there.

HECTARE: metric unit of area, equivalent to 2.47 acres.

HOME RANGE: the area that an animal patrols regularly.

IMBABURA: small portable stove.

JUVENILE: a physically immature individual.

KILO (KILOGRAM): metric unit for mass and weight, equivalent to 2.2 pounds

MACHETE: a large, heavy knife used to cut down brush.

MANIOC: a major food crop grown in the tropics for its starchy roots, which are soaked to remove toxins before consumption.

MARCHÉ: French word for marketplace.

METER: metric unit of length, equivalent to 1.09 yards.

MONTANE RAIN FOREST: rain forest that exists in a cool, mountainous region.

PLANT TUBER: a fleshy root.

PRIMATE: the order of mammals comprising humans, apes, monkeys, tarsiers, and lemurs.

RAIN FOREST: a lush, green, leafy forest that receives over 100 inches of rain annually.

SOCIAL GROOMING: the practice of searching for dirt and parasites in another animal's fur, providing beneficial social contact.

SPOOR: the trail left behind by a wild animal, including its tracks and droppings.

SWEAT FLIES: small, non-biting flies that are attracted to water or perspiration.

TARMAC: a road or runway built by pouring tar over crushed stones.

WATERSHED: an area of land from which water drains, forming a watercourse or a body of water.

WILDLIFE CENSUS: a population count of the existing species of wild animals in an area.

Turaco Feather

VERTICAL DISTRIBUTION OF PRIMATE SPECIES
IN KIBIRA NATIONAL PARK

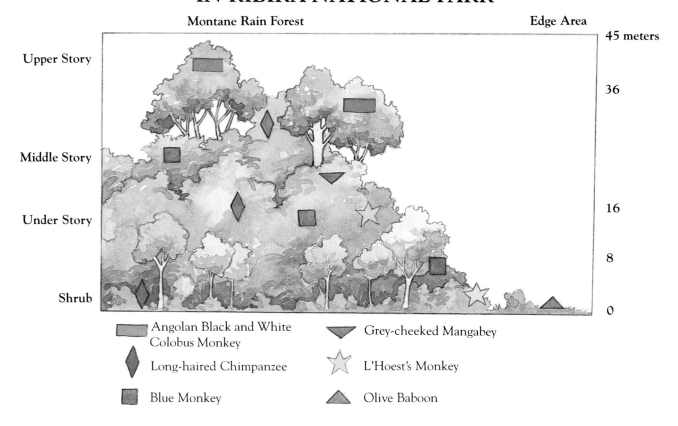

Montane Rain Forest   Edge Area

Upper Story — 45 meters, 36

Middle Story

Under Story — 16, 8

Shrub — 0

Symbol	Species	Symbol	Species
▭	Angolan Black and White Colobus Monkey	▽	Grey-cheeked Mangabey
◆	Long-haired Chimpanzee	★	L'Hoest's Monkey
▪	Blue Monkey	▲	Olive Baboon

ANIMAL INDEX

Long-horned Beetle